E 27966

B
SALER-
NO-SON

Salerno-Sonnenberg, Nadja.

Nadja, on my way.

$16.37

DATE DUE	BORROWER'S NAME	ROOM NO.

E 27966

B
SALER-
NO-SON

Salerno-Sonnenberg, Nadja.

Nadja, on my way.

Nadja

ON MY WAY

NADJA

CROWN PUBLISHERS, INC., NEW YORK

ON MY WAY

Nadja Salerno-Sonnenberg

Published by Crown Publishers, Inc., 225 Park Avenue South, New York, New
York 10003 and represented in Canada by the Canadian MANDA Group.
CROWN is a trademark of Crown Publishers, Inc.
Printed in the U.S.A.
Lyrics from "Graduation Day," by Joe Sherman and Noel Sherman, copyright
© 1956, renewed 1984, by Erasmus Music, were reprinted in chapter nine
with the kind permission of Erasmus Music, care of the Songwriters Guild of
America.
Jacket photos copyright © 1989 by Janette Beckman.

Library of Congress Cataloging-in-Publication Data
Salerno-Sonnenberg, Nadja. Nadja, on my way / Nadja Salerno-Sonnenberg.
Summary: The talented and flamboyant violinist describes her childhood, education and training at Juilliard, and concert performances around the world.
1. Salerno-Sonnenberg, Nadja—Juvenile literature. 2. Violinists—Biography—Juvenile literature. [1. Salerno-Sonnenberg, Nadja. 2. Violinists.
   3. Musicians.] I. Title.
ML3930.S18A3   1989   787.2'092—dc20   [B]   89-7661   [92]

ISBN 0-517-57392-X
    0-517-57391-1 (lib. bdg.)

10 9 8 7 6 5 4 3 2 1

First Edition

Contents

Illustrations

Editor's Acknowledgment

As a young violinist, Nadja Salerno-Sonnenberg is necessarily busy living her life: playing concerts, studying, and recording. It would not have occurred to her to write a book about her life. The suggestion came from Betty Prashker, Editor-in-Chief of Crown Publishers.

I want to thank Laurence Tucker of Columbia Artists Management, Mary Lou Falcone of M.L. Falcone Public Relations, and greatest thanks to Nadja Salerno-Sonnenberg herself for agreeing to this project.

I interviewed Miss Salerno-Sonnenberg and prepared a first draft of the manuscript. She read it and added new material. This process was repeated several times over the period of a year as photographs, chapter epigrams, and discography were added, and the manuscript evolved.

This book was written in the hope that it will interest and encourage young musicians and be an enjoyment for the audience of Nadja Salerno-Sonnenberg's art.

David Allender

Nadja

ON MY WAY

Overture

Don't play as if it were a habit! Maybe you've played
well, but you can still play badly—it's much easier.
Don't ever think you've succeeded. Always try to do
better—otherwise drop dead.

—Arturo Toscanini

This is something I know for a fact: You have to work hardest
for the thing you love most. And when it's music that you love,
you're in for the fight of your life.

It starts when your blood fills with music and you know
you can't live without it. Every day brings a challenge to learn
as much as possible and to play even better than you did the day
before.

You may want to achieve fame and glory, or you may want
to play for fun. But whenever you fall in love with music, you'll
never sit still again.

Music is more important than we will ever know. Great
music can pull you right out of your chair. It can make you cry,
or laugh, or feel a way you've never felt before. It can make you
remember the first person you loved, or it can make you want
to kill someone. Music has that power.

Just imagine a world without music. What would you whistle when you walked down the street? How could you make a movie? How could you have a ball game without an organist leading the crowd when you're down by a run in the ninth?

You could be the most successful doctor in the world, but if you never turn on the radio, never go to a concert, never sing in the shower, never saw *The King and I*—then you can't be a total, fulfilled human being. It's impossible.

When you realize how vital music is, you realize a musician's fight is quite a noble, heroic endeavor. It didn't always seem that way to me. There was a time, years ago, when I felt discouraged and it seemed selfish to put so much time into music. Being a musician didn't seem as useful to others as being a surgeon, or even a good politician.

But I came to understand that it's a great, great gift to help people forget their everyday life and be uplifted. And better than uplifted, to be inspired; that's what music can do. It's important to us all, and I'm proud to put mind and muscle into recording, concerts, teaching, and studying: into being a musician.

Emotionally, music has brought me an enormous amount of joy and an enormous amount of despair and frustration. Because of music, I have learned what a battle is. I've won most, but not all—not by a long shot.

It's a reward to see people affected at my concerts and, after concerts, hearing from them. Mothers have come backstage and said, "My son saw you on TV and he decided to play the violin."

During a master class in Aspen, a young girl played the Bruch G minor Concerto for me. I had played the Bruch there, and she played it exactly the way I did. I was thrilled and embarrassedly happy to have affected a young violinist that way.

Yet I will never feel satisfied because there are always many goals ahead. Some days I can't believe I've come as far as I have—and how much further I want to go.

I wrote this book about my life work, and this book may also be about yours. Being a musician is never easy. It takes guts or stupidity to walk onstage and play the violin. You may have a bad day in front of thousands.

No matter what happens throughout your life, though, the music is always there. Friends can run away, but Brahms never will.

And he's listening.

Duet

Violin playing is a combination
of engineering and choreography;
but what emerges must come
from the heart.

—David Oistrakh

I was born in Rome and raised in my grandparents' apartment, just a few blocks from the Vatican. My mother, Josephine Salerno, played piano. My brother Eric sang. Grandfather John Salerno (always known to us as Papa John) was a trumpet player. Nanny, grandmother Rose, cooked and played kazoo.

Mama had a friend who taught violin to beginners, so the violin was stuck under my chin when I was five and that was that.

I can't say there was love at first sight. More than anything, I wanted to make music—but with this? For a beginner, the violin is almost impossible to hold correctly, and once you do it's uncomfortable. Some prize. Then, playing a tune you could whistle in a second is like leading the invasion of Normandy.

If I'd had a choice about an instrument, I might have chosen the piano. You want an A, press down a key and there's A.

Getting an A or any solid tone out of the violin takes almost endless practice. But even then, the nightmare's just begun. Making music out of those tones is no spring picnic. For one thing, there are no frets on a violin fingerboard as there are on a guitar. A violinist has to memorize the notes by touch.

Whoever invented the instrument probably went on to invent the rack, Chinese water torture, and tooth decay. A violin is a hard piece of wood that scars your neck, your right hand draws a thin bow, and your left fingers are half-curled on the fingerboard pressing down metal strings. Nothing about the violin is natural, comfortable, easy, or graceful.

There are difficulties galore playing any instrument well. But for just plain never-ending drudgery, the violin has to be right up at the top of the list. Fortunately, the violin teacher was the best-smelling man in Italy.

The kind of music teacher any beginner should have is someone who isn't too strict, who smiles and makes jokes and tells you you're good. You need someone who makes learning the instrument fun because that's really what music is truly about.

Signore Antonio Marchetti, a violinist with the Italian Radio Symphony, was everything I could want. He wore the most fabulous cologne. I could even put up with the violin just to sit next to him and *mmmm,* inhale that Aqua di Selva.

"Nadja," Signore Marchetti said after I'd learned the basics, "elbow up! Keep the violin high, and our next lesson we'll start something special!"

What he meant by "something special" was a new piece. It was called *Czardas* by Alberto Curci, played with open strings; but it had a piano part as well.

When people came to eat at our house, they didn't just get a meal. After having the most fabulous food you can imagine, we would sit around the piano and start right in. Eric would sing, Mama would play, Papa John would play; polkas, arias, waltzes, I mean anything.

After I learned *Czardas,* Mama and I were to play a duet after one of our family dinners. I should add that I was not going to be the headliner. Who wants to hear the kid who just started to play the violin? I was going to be the evening's opening act—when everybody still had dessert and coffee to keep them happy.

I played *Czardas* for my teacher every week in our lesson for two weeks . . . three weeks . . . four weeks . . . five weeks.

Finally, he said, *"Bene! Sei pronto!"* That meant Okay, now you're ready to play it with the piano.

Signore Marchetti was wrong. I wasn't at all ready for what happened next.

Mama's part was equally easy. There was a two-bar vamp and then the violin squeaks in with an *eeh, eeh, eeh.*

So Mama played her vamp; *um-cha, um-cha, um-cha, um-cha.* Then I came in *eeh, eeh, eeh* . . .

And there was music! I was playing my part and she was playing her part and together it was harmony!

I started to cry and couldn't stop. I could only say how beautiful, what a beautiful thing we had done. It was the first time I made music, right there in the living room, rehearsing with my mama.

I pulled her back to the piano so we could play it again and again. That was the moment for me; the thrill of making music went straight into my blood.

Then came the night of our performance. We played our duet and I looked at the people and heard clapping. Relatives were smiling and saying, "Oh, isn't she cute!"

Wow, I thought, I can do this and people *appreciate* it. That went straight into my bloodstream as well.

Even after that night, I still didn't like practicing. And having a musician for a mother didn't make it easier. I'd be playing and she would tell me, "That's out of tune."

I'd say, "So what?"

"So you have to play it in tune."

"Why?"

"Because that's the thing to do," she'd say. "If you're going to play it out of tune, don't play it. A lot of people can play it out of tune. You have to play it *in* tune."

I remember once I was in my room practicing *Twinkle,*

Twinkle Little Star. I just didn't feel like it so I purposely made sixteen mistakes. At the time, this seemed a very clever thing to do. It wasn't, because naturally my mother heard me.

She came into the room and spanked me sixteen times. "If you're not going to do your best," she said, "don't do it at all."

Playing in tune took constant practice and that was hard. It was hard to always play at my best. But, boy, the final result, making music, was just fantastic for me.

A violin can be the most incredible sound you've ever heard. Through a composer's music it can express everything from the wildest joy to the deepest pain. The sound of the violin compares only to a singer's voice, but in one way the violin has an advantage.

A singer has to pause for breath. A violinist never has to stop. You can draw the bow up, then down, upbow, downbow, upbow, downbow—there never has to be a pause. Any singer will run out of breath, but a violinist will never run out of bow.

Leaving Italy

Yankees! America! Hot dog!" It was 1969, the year that man would walk on the moon, and we were moving to America.

For the rest of my family, it wasn't the first time. They had all lived in America before. Mama and Eric were born there; but it was a new country for me and I owed it to Signore Marchetti.

By the time I was eight, I had gotten better and better at the violin. Signore Marchetti told my mother and grandparents, "Nadja has promise, and I've taught her everything I can."

If they were interested, and if they were serious, he said, America was the place for a violinist to study. They thought it over, discussed it, and in the end, we started packing.

The trip took Nanny and me ten days on the luxury liner *Michelangelo*. The others went by plane. I must say I was more excited about going to America than sad to leave Italy. Even the language was exciting. Everyone in my family spoke English, and they taught me my first words: "Yankees," "America," and "hot dog." I think I shouted my vocabulary the entire way to the United States.

I remember well the sight of the Statue of Liberty as we came into New York Harbor. My grandmother explained its meaning, that it was a symbol of hope and opportunity, and she told me about her life in America.

In the 1920s, Nanny and Papa John worked in the clothing factories of South Philadelphia when they were just teenagers. At that time, the workers were treated like dirt by their bosses. There was nothing to protect the workers' rights, and my grandmother joined the fight for unions.

The factory owners tried to stop her, and Nanny's friends suddenly wouldn't speak to her. Still she fought for what was right. A union was established, and the same people who deserted her wanted to be friends again.

"How could you forgive them?" I asked her.

She just said, "It was all right. They weren't as strong as I was."

A typical Salerno woman. All Salerno women are great fighters and workers. Sometimes much to our dismay; the women usually end up doing all the work.

I'll always have a boundless respect for Nanny and Mama. My father left the family when I was three months old. Nanny practically raised my brother and me while my mother and grandfather earned a living. Nadja Rose Sonnenberg was my name from birth; I added the Salerno to honor my mother's parents and my Italian heritage as well.

The *Michelangelo* finally docked in New York City, and Nanny and I took a train to Philadelphia. I was luckier than a lot of people coming to this country for the first time. We didn't have to walk around in a daze saying, "Excuse me, where's the bathroom?"

My grandmother's sister Angela lived in Philly, and Angela had a son with a wife and kids. So Eric and I had American cousins to play with, and we all had spaghetti and meatballs at their house every Sunday night.

With English being spoken on all sides, I was able to add to my first three words by learning at home. Like playing the violin in tune, English was drilled in. I had an accent for a while and then that went away. I still curse in Italian, and I dream in Italian sometimes. But I feel very American, and quite proud to be one.

My family rented a place in Camden, New Jersey (in better days, home to the Victor Talking Machine Company where Caruso, Kreisler, Toscanini, and many others made early recordings), until a house was found in Cherry Hill, a Philadelphia suburb. Our neighborhood was on a dead-end street, a street with nine other houses. The backyard was huge and my grandfather began digging it up for a garden. Our house was big too, but not quite big enough for the five of us. It had four bedrooms, so I shared with Mama.

The cul-de-sac was like a little city. There was a concession stand across the street, where five cents could get you enough candy for fifteen cavities. And right next to the stand was a Little League park.

"Nooooo-batterbatterbatter! Lessssgo, lessssgo! Chucker in there, Eddie-baby!" Not since the outdoor operas in Rome had I seen and heard anything as beautiful as baseball: the three-run homer, the wild pitch, the stolen base, the chatter, and the cheers.

Since it was one of the first English words out of my mouth, the Yankees were (and still are) my major league team. I also loved the Dallas Cowboys because Roger Staubach and Lance Alworth were the cutest guys in football. The Phillies I could not care less about. But I rooted hard for the Flyers when they were going for their third straight Stanley Cup, and the Eagles when Tom Dempsey was their kicker. He had half a foot and half a hand, yet Dempsey was one of the great NFL kickers of all time. Very inspirational guy.

In a short time, we were settled in. Mama got a job as a music teacher in the Philadelphia public school system. Papa John went back to the factory, sewing pockets on jackets, and put a little band together to make money on the side.

He was quite a good trumpeter, my grandfather. His band came to be in big demand at bar mitzvahs. For an Italian, Papa John sure could play *Hava Nagilah* great.

Lessons

Never miss an opportunity of hearing a good opera.

—Robert Schumann

I didn't learn how to read music at a music school. My grandfather taught me.

Papa John Salerno was the strictest teacher I ever had. When we came to America, and for many years after, the solfeggio class was in my grandparents' bedroom every Tuesday. He had me read through a little exercise book by Pasquale Bono; sing *do, re, me, fa, sol, la, si, do*; and learn the meaning of notes and musical time.

Rhythm was the hardest thing for me about sight-reading. As I learned, I could pretty much play notes on a page, but rhythmically I had problems. Maybe I just don't have a mathematical way of thinking; I tend to be more emotional and instinctive than strictly analytical. Whatever the reason, counting and dividing beats came with great effort. And great detection.

Reading music is like solving a mystery. When I look at a

new piece of music, all the notes look the same. Some are higher on the staff, some are lower, but it's just a page full of black dots.

To be a musician, you have to be able to tell which dots are important: which dots represent the climax of the phrase and which dots connect one phrase to another.

Sometimes you'll play through a piece and see, "Oh, that's a beautiful phrase. Let me do that again." Through detective work, you'll find phrases throughout a piece of music.

My grandfather gave me many things, more than I was aware of at the time. Papa John wasn't a great musician with a great soul and great mind. He was an honest, simple man who worked in a factory and played the horn; yet the man could sight-read like the best musicians around. Any clef, anything. I've yet to see the equal of the training he received as a kid in Sicily.

Perhaps above all, Papa John game me a love of opera. Every Saturday in America "Texaco Presents" was on and my grandfather and I would sit by the radio and listen to The Metropolitan Opera Broadcasts from New York City. He would explain every single thing to the point where I could barely hear the music.

"Now she's trying to get away," he'd say. "Now he took out a knife . . ." I would get so immersed in the story line, in the totality of opera.

For my money, opera is the most magnificent form of art man has invented. There's everything. You've got costumes, you've got a story—talk about great stories! It's more than a symphony because you've got these incredible sounds which are the human voice.

I fell in love with singing as I would with baseball. But while I can play left field with the best of them (at least the best of them playing softball in Central Park), unfortunately I can't really sing. I mean, *My Funny Valentine,* fine, but an aria from *La Bohème,* forget it.

Still, I think singing when I play the violin. If I were to sing a passage I'm playing, where would I take my breath? How does this line of music make a sentence with a beginning, middle, and end? That is my instinctual way of playing music, from love of opera, and my grandfather's lessons, when I was very young.

If you don't have an Italian grandfather, but would like to learn about opera, I wouldn't advise you to start with something like *Lohengrin* or *Tristan und Isolde*. They're Wagner and I love them, but they're six hours long and there's a guy in front of a rock singing about a god. It's like puh-leeese!

Start with *Carmen*. Georges Bizet's *Carmen* is opera's Hit Parade. After you see it, you won't know which tune to whistle first. Great story, very passionate, a lot of action.

The first opera I saw onstage, at an age when I knew what was really going on, was Richard Strauss's *Salome*. It's a biblical story about the psycho stepdaughter of King Herod.

The story goes like this: Herod is keeping John the Baptist prisoner, and Salome falls in love with him. He rejects her. She does a veil dance and requests John's beheading. Her request is granted, and they march in with John's head on a platter.

Salome kisses the head, falls to the floor in ecstasy, and Herod orders his soldiers to squash her with their shields.

That's how it ends. The kettledrums go *bu-rumm, bu-rumm,* and the curtain falls and it's over.

I was fourteen at the time, and for me it was the operatic equivalent of *The Texas Chain Saw Massacre*. It completely blew my mind.

Anything by Verdi or Puccini, any of the romantic operas such as *La Traviata, Otello, Tosca,* and *La Bohème* are great things to see. Then there are serious and comic operas by Rossini and Mozart such as *Cenerentola* and *Magic Flute* which are absolutely gorgeous.

And opera isn't the only theatrical form of music that's worth knowing. Ballet is beautiful too, though I learned that as an art form, it isn't enough for me. There are music and wonderful things to watch, but I always feel bad for the ballerinas. It's like they're all mute. I feel bad that they can't say anything.

You may feel differently. Two of the most famous ballets, *Nutcracker* and *Coppélia,* are great introductions. I can't imagine you'd be bored at either one.

In any kind of art, you'll find the things you like by trial and error. Go to concerts, galleries, museums, listen to the radio, rent videos—the important thing is to stay alert and look for beauty everywhere.

You'll learn from it all.

Curtis

Even though my mother and grandfather were working, there was never enough money to go around. There were six of us to feed, including the cat. All the money was spent on bills and on food.

Nanny, being the wonderful cook she was, could make the most incredible meal out of three eggs. I was never a starving child. We just didn't have money to go out and buy things, yet I never felt poor.

I was living in a pretty nice neighborhood, and we were in a beautiful house. Toys and new clothes were the icing we never had.

Until I was eighteen, all the clothes I wore were from garage sales. Everything but underwear, even shoes. Every single thing I wore some other kid had worn first. My brother and I had to make our own toys. In a way, it was good not being given things, because if you really want something, you make it yourself.

Once, when I was about eleven, the teachers were on strike and Mama was on the picket line. I had gotten very interested in chess and begged her for a set, the $5.99 plastic kind with a paper board. With all the love in her heart, she said we just couldn't affort it.

So I made it. I got a cardboard box, cut out the figure of each piece, made my board, used some black and white paint— done. I had my chess set.

A normal day when we first arrived in Cherry Hill would start at six in the morning with an hour of practice. I would do exercises, scales, all the usual things. Sometimes I'd be so sleepy I'd doze off with the violin in my lap. When the hour was up, my mother would come in and say, "Okay, come on, time to go to school."

Back in Rome, I had walked to school, Catholic school, in the silly costume we had to wear. But my first school in America, Joyce Kilmer Elementary (named for the poet who wrote about a tree), had a school bus. The floor was sticky, it stank of fumes and kids, the jabbering was deafening. I loved that bus.

Being alone most of the time, practicing and studying, is a price you pay to be a musician. Since I spent so many hours by myself, a bus ride with friends was a treat. Much later, when I toured Europe by bus with the Juilliard Orchestra, everyone complained about the nine-hour rides. Not me. I had the time of my life.

When the bus brought me home after school, I had to practice again. My mother would come home from work and sit in this ugly green lounge chair that the cat had sharpened her nails on. It was the most putrid-looking chair in the universe. My mother would sit in that chair with a crossword puzzle and listen to me practice for two hours.

She'd say, "It's out of tune, do it again . . . that's not good, do it again . . . you're rushing, do it again . . ." And when that was done, I'd have to do my homework.

Now, I was never a scholar and fortunately my mother

never enforced the goal of high grades. She realized I had the violin to practice and how much can a kid do? No parent can reasonably expect straight A's while the kid is practicing three or four hours a day. And maybe deep down Mama never felt A's were so important.

She wasn't happy when I came home with straight D's, but I could hear her in the other room saying, "Well, at least she didn't fail."

When it came to math, I just simply told her, "Look. I don't like it. I'm not good at it. I just don't understand it."

She said, "Okay. Do the best you can. Please try and do the best you can. It would be wonderful if you came home with B's. We would be very happy."

Finally, after my homework was done, I could go out and play. I had made friends on the bus, and it was so frustrating to hear the other kids outside all that time.

"Can Nadja come out and play?"

"No, not yet."

Some days I had a lot of homework. Some days I didn't. But I always went out and played.

The other kids played four hours. I played two hours. And when I went out I *played:* kickball and softball and, as we got a little older, made-up games like Star Trek. One kid knew math and chemistry, he liked those things, so he got to be Mr. Spock. He knew words like "atmosphere."

I was Kirk.

At first, we were using pencils for phasers, but then all the other kids went out and bought their plastic Star Trek junk. Phasers, tricorders, communicators . . . they even came with plastic belts.

And of course, being Kirk, I wanted my own. I was the captain! I had to have a phaser.

So I went in and said, "Mama, I want—"

"I'm sorry, we can't afford it."

"Everyone else has one. Why can't I? Why can't I have a phaser? Everybody has a phaser, I don't have a phaser. I'm Captain Kirk! It's not fair!"

I know my mother felt sorry for me, but I wasn't the type to feel sorry for myself. I drew the shape of a phaser on a piece of two-by-four. My Uncle Dom was a carpenter, and he cut it out on his power saw. Then I sanded it, painted it, I made my phaser. I made everything, and it turned out the kids liked my stuff better.

I didn't hate my mother or blame her or feel jealous of the other kids. If we didn't have the money, I would just think of another way. It's a quality that has carried me through my entire life. Now, more than ever, I need that determination: "Okay, I will find a way. I will do it."

Throughout our first months in America, Mama was busy finding a place that taught violin. She knew someone who worked at the Curtis Institute of Music—one of the best music colleges in the country—so she went and asked for guidance.

"I don't know any good teachers," she said. "Where can I go?"

It was arranged that I would come in and play for the violin teachers at Curtis. I didn't know it was an important thing. I met Mama at the school; she said, "Take the violin out and play." So I did.

I played my *Czardas* and a couple of other things, then I left the room while Mama stayed behind to talk to the teachers.

It didn't cost money to study at Curtis. In fact, unlike other schools, you couldn't pay to get in. It was free for anyone they felt was good enough to be there.

The violin faculty members at Curtis liked me. Even though I was eight, they decided to take me on. Curtis was a college. I was a *small* eight-year-old. Everyone else at Curtis was at least seventeen. I came up to all the other students' knees.

When I went for my first lesson at Curtis, I couldn't open the doors to get in. There was a heavy wooden door followed by a heavier iron door. To get inside, I had to wait until somebody came out.

I didn't understand English too well, so being there was pretty frightening. But all the kids treated me as if I were their little daughter. I just blindly followed their knees to class. I didn't understand a thing that was going on.

At the end of the school year, Curtis held auditions and ten more little kids were accepted. Curtis started a preparatory division in the fall of 1970, and my days on the Joyce Kilmer school bus were over. But my days as Dennis the Menace were just beginning.

Debut

Forget tradition. Dismiss the idea that you must try to
play such and such a work just as so and so plays it.
Do not think of style! Concentrate quite simply and
honestly on putting your whole heart and soul into the
task of making the music you are playing live.

—Leopold Auer

The Curtis Institute of Music gave me my basic training as a
violinist. At the time, Curtis taught the Galamian Violin
Method, and Ivan Galamian himself was associated with the
school.

Galamian's students included Michael Rabin, Jaime La-
redo, Itzhak Perlman as a kid, Pinchas Zukerman, and many
other well-known players. When I was young, Galamian was
probably the world's most respected figure in violin teaching.

Curtis actually has quite a rich history of legendary violin
teachers. Carl Flesch taught at Curtis when it opened in 1924.
Leopold Auer and Efrem Zimbalist both taught there. Galamian
taught in his New York City apartment and all the Curtis kids
traveled to play for him.

I can't say that I learned much from Galamian. My most
vivid memory is watching his burning cigarette turn into one

long ash. Then he'd move his arm ver-r-r-y slo-o-o-wly over a beautiful rug to the ashtray. I believe he was showing me what a strong bow arm he had.

I would play for him every now and then so he could see my improvement, but mostly I studied at the school itself with Galamian's assistant, Jascha Brodsky, and *his* assistant, a young Japanese girl named Yumi Ninomiya.

The Curtis Institute was in an old mansion on Rittenhouse Square. Inside, it was a dark kind of medieval-looking place once you made it past the doors; a big fireplace in the lobby, ancient carpets, a mahogany desk where the receptionist, Mrs. Brunson, sat.

After I stopped being awestruck with the grandeur, I became a terrible terror, getting into trouble for everything you can possibly imagine—roller-skating on the Persian rugs, dropping water bombs off the roof, cutting up in class.

And when they opened the prep division and let ten other kids in, I showed the new kids the ropes. I had already been there a year. I was the hardened con. I knew every nook and cranny where a kid could hide from teachers.

When we weren't hiding, the academic experience for us preps was pretty unusual. In fairness, no doubt putting together that type of program was pretty difficult. After I left, the school stopped having a prep division altogether, and these days young players take academic classes outside Curtis.

There was an English class that had me; a girl from the Philippines who became my best friend—Cecile Licad (now a world-renowned concert pianist who studied at Curtis with Mieczyslaw Horszowski, Seymour Lipkin, and Rudolf Serkin); an Israeli violinist; a Japanese pianist; and one American boy who was such a tightwad and whiner we all hated him. There's always one in every class: "But I disagree, teacher!" with his hand waving back and forth.

Since most of the class barely spoke English, our teacher decided we would read *Macbeth*.

The Israeli violinist would start reading aloud slowly, in a thick accent, "If . . . it . . . were daa-*done* . . . wuh-wuh-when 'tis done . . . [long pause] 'twere well . . . done quig-*quickly* . . .

if the . . . [longer pause, tightwad shouts, "Let me read, teacher!"] uhh-sss-*assination* could . . . trrr-*trammel* up . . . the . . . con . . . the . . . con . . ." and our books would fall from our fingers as we slipped into deep comas.

Our chemistry class was on the same chapter for two years. We're talking about musicians here who could not convert Fahrenheit into centigrade. We just couldn't do it. All we could grasp was thirty-two equals zero. After that, we were completely lost.

The teachers would just look determined and say, "Well, if you don't get it this year, you'll learn it next year."

There wasn't any type of gym class at first, but it finally dawned on people that perhaps the kids should have some kind of physical outlet. So they started a yoga class.

We were nine years old—we didn't want to do yoga, we wanted to play baseball. We would have been much happier getting blood on our knees and dirt up our noses than squeaking around on those plastic mats. I feel the same today. The brilliant Yehudi Menuhin is an advocate of yoga for musicians; personally, though, I'm happier in a pickup game of football.

It wasn't all so bad, I must admit. One of my favorite things was cutting class and going into the organ pipes. I saved the best place to hide for myself.

Curtis Hall had organ pipes on the walls and ceiling. For workmen to get into the pipes for repairs, there was a little entrance hole to crawl through.

I swear to this day they must be finding Spiderman comic books and potato chip bags up in those pipes. I would sit up there for hours and read and eat and sleep. Then college kids would come in and practice the organ.

The sound of an organ playing fortissimo is completely deafening when you stand next to the pipes. I was inside the pipes and the sound just didn't bother me. It was a very physical way to hear a fugue.

Almost in spite of myself, I managed to learn some very good things, especially in back of the Curtis Orchestra string section.

The school had orchestra rehearsals twice a week, every Thursday night and Saturday morning. The Saturday rehearsal was led by whichever guest conductor was in town to conduct the Philadelphia Orchestra.

Due to that, I had the chance to work under the greatest conductors in the word. I even got to be the translator for Riccardo Muti.

To prepare for this day with the guest artist we would rehearse the same piece Thursday night with William Smith, associate conductor of the Philadelphia Orchestra.

Thursday-night rehearsal was from seven to ten. Sometimes longer. I couldn't go home by myself at that hour, so Mama would come after work. She'd sit in the lobby for three hours until I was out of orchestra. I felt very bad about that. To give her something to do, I made crossword puzzles.

They were very hard to make up. You had to think up the clues, the answer, then draw all those squares. Not too long ago, I found out that my mother never did one of them. She thought they were cute and saved them all in a trunk.

Orchestra gave a whole new meaning to practicing. When you play an instrument such as the violin, you can't accompany yourself. There are unaccompanied pieces, but they're a small part of the repertory. You practice by yourself and when you finally hear how your part combines to make music, it's electrifying.

It's like this. Say you put on 250 pounds and become an offensive lineman in the NFL. A big part of your job is pass protection for the quarterback; so you practice pass-blocking against a defender. You take a little step back then, *whap*, block the defender. Step, *whap,* step, *whap*, that's how you practice. What the heck is this? you might ask yourself, Is this playing football? Then you get in a game. The ball is snapped, all five of you on the line step back, *whap,* step, *whap*, and the quarterback hits the wide receiver for a touchdown. You only see the value of all that hard practicing when the pieces fit together, when your stepping and whapping help win a game.

Playing well as a string section was like being on a team that won the Super Bowl. It gave me something new to strive for as a player. And familiarity with orchestral accompaniment also prepared me for my debut as a soloist.

One of the great benefits of orchestra work is that you develop a little orchestra right in your head. When I'm home and practicing a concerto, in my mind I hear each part of the orchestral score. I hear the clarinet part, the bassoon part, the strings, every single part. And while I'm playing my part, I'm grunting the orchestra's. I'll be playing along beautifully and going, "Grunt, grunt, grunt . . ." at the same time. In my head, I'm hearing how it will sound, but if someone were listening they would think something was wrong with me.

My debut came when I was ten, on July 28, 1971. The Philadelphia Orchestra had held concert auditions for any young player living within a fifty-mile radius of the city. I fit the description, so I auditioned and won.

There were three other winners: another violinist and a cellist, both eleven-year-olds, and a twelve-year-old pianist. The four of us were to play one morning concert each at the old Robin Hood Dell in Fairmount Park, now the Mann Music Center—the orchestra's summer home. I was to play the Bach Concerto in A minor, first movement, and my family bought me my first new dress for the occasion.

William Smith was the conductor of these concerts. The organizers bused in huge audiences of kids to the park grounds. I couldn't have been happier. The only thing I was worried about was tripping over the wires on stage. My mother was a wreck. Everybody was a wreck except me.

I was going to play Bach with the Philadelphia Orchestra in front of twelve thousand people at ten-thirty in the morning, but I knew as long as I didn't trip, everything would be okay.

William Smith came onstage and announced what I was to play and introduced the piece.

"Bach," he said, "lived a long, long time ago, and he had a lot of kids. He was an organist and a great composer and he wrote this concerto for violin and orchestra.

"A concerto is a piece of music with orchestra and a soloist. The violinist is like the star of the piece. The orchestra is accompanying the violin, but you will hear the violin playing certain themes, and I want you to listen for those themes when the orchestra plays them. Sometimes the orchestra and violin will play the themes together, and that's called ensemble."

When the piece was over, he turned to the audience and said, "Did you hear the basses playing the same theme as the violin?" and thousands of kids shouted, *"Yeah!!!"*

I remember looking out at the audience and not seeing the end of the people. I couldn't believe that all of them could hear me. I didn't know from sound systems and amps. I couldn't see the last row of people, and that was awesome to me. But I could see a friend of mine in the front row and I waved at her.

What did I know? Nothing. I was on stage for four minutes, went *eeh, eeh, eeh,* and then I was off. Two years later, I won the orchestra prize again and played the Mendelssohn Concerto in the Academy of Music. Same thing: la-de-da, isn't this fun?

It wasn't until I reached college that I learned how hard all this was, and I started getting nervous about concerts, about the idea of performing, and excellence in playing. Now I have dreams (more like nightmares actually) about going onstage and forgetting the first note.

All in all, I received a lot from my years at Curtis, but I also gradually began to develop some bad playing habits. I hope this doesn't sound cranky, but the Galamian Method put players into a mold. You learned pieces in a certain order and you used these fingerings and held the bow this way.

That worked fine when I first came to Curtis. And it worked for thousands of musicians. But I resisted the system. I kept asking "Why" and my teachers didn't like that, so I just stopped learning from them. I had my own ideas, and began doing things my own way.

It wasn't the right thing to do, but something big was happening. I was growing up.

Juilliard

You must be sensitive to rhythm, melody, harmony,
to the atmosphere which sounds create, to be
thrilled with the linking of two chords, as with the
harmony of two colors.

—Maurice Ravel

Starting when I was thirteen, I studied in France every September. That still left summertime for fooling around and figuring things out.

One summer I wanted to know how houses were built. The first thing I figured is that building one wasn't going to be cheap. I needed big bucks.

Papa John gave me two dollars' allowance every Friday. He barely got in the door before I grabbed him. And on my birthday, with aunts and uncles all over the place, I'd get five dollars here, ten dollars there . . . I'd make almost a hundred dollars on my birthday with all those relatives.

Then I would go around the house, "Do you want me to shine your shoes? Can I wash the car? Can I make a little extra money?"

I put it all in a little box I made and saved for a long, long time. I kept a chart that showed how much money I had socked away. I bought concrete, I spent two hundred dollars on wood, I drew up plans. My Uncle Dom helped me again.

Since Eric was older, of course, he didn't help at all. We were typical brother and sister. You know, "Get out of my face! I hate you! Nyah, nyah, nyah!"

When I finally had my supplies, I dug up dirt for the foundation close to my grandfather's garden. He kept an eye on me and on his tomatoes. I mixed up the cement, put in cinder blocks, and secured two-by-fours all around with special nails. Next I poured cement inside the boards and nailed plywood on top. That made my floor.

Then I put up the walls, nailed down support beams and built a roof, hammered a door frame together and hinged a door, added windows; the whole thing on my own. Figuring out how to build my house was the interesting part. I hardly went into the thing after I finished it, even though I practically could have moved in. But while it was going up, I couldn't sleep at night. All I could think about was what I would accomplish tomorrow. Fortunately, the last nail was in before I had to leave.

I was going for a three-week festival at the Académie de Musique Maurice Ravel in the south of France, right on the Basque border. It was a beautiful place in the town of St. Jean de Luz.

Philippe Entremont was the festival director. He and I became close, like father and daughter, and have remained friends and colleagues to this day. He taught piano with Gaby Casadesus, Pierre Bernac was head of the voice department, and Christian Ferras was the violin teacher.

The best musicians are not always the best teachers. Jascha Heifetz, probably the greatest violinist of the century, was one of the worst teachers in history.

"Watch, listen. Play it like me," Heifetz would say. How could anyone learn while failing to play like Heifetz?

Ferras was a very good teacher and a very good violinist, but he was mean to everyone. He was also built like a linebacker. You didn't want to make him mad but it was hard not to: he had no patience and a surly nature. He made all the students cry, including me. But never in class. I'd hold it back and cry later.

In a strange way he gave me a boost. Though he tried not to show it, I could tell he liked me. And being liked by such a lout gave me confidence.

When I went in 1975 for the first lesson of my second year there, Ferras said, in his usual straightforward way, "You haven't improved at all! Who are you studying with? This is no good. You must leave your teacher!"

He spoke to my mother and she said, "Well, maybe we have to move her on from Curtis if she hasn't improved." So that September, I left Curtis after six years there as a student. Simple as that.

The idea of becoming a professional musician wasn't a real ambition at that point in my life. At the age of fourteen, I wanted to be a ballplayer or an astronaut. I wasn't concerned about improvement in my playing.

Later, when I was seventeen and around kids wanting to be concert artists, I thought, "Yes, that's what I want! That's what I want to do with my life!" But before then, I either wasn't thinking about having a life in music, or I was just never doubting that I would. It certainly wasn't something to *fret* about.

Mama got busy again, and through the suggestion of some friends, I went to New York City and auditioned for Miss Dorothy DeLay. If accepted, I would have private lessons with Miss DeLay and classes at the Pre-College Division of the Juilliard School of Music.

Dorothy DeLay was once an assistant to Ivan Galamian, but had long since gone on her own. By the time I auditioned for her, she was already well established. She had taught Perlman and he was already way up there, and she had taught the likes of Shlomo Mintz and others.

I had never heard of her, but I sure had heard of Juilliard. Just the name was as magical as saying "Carnegie Hall." Audition for them? I practiced like crazy.

The Pre-College at Juilliard is for kids eight to eighteen.

Classes are just once a week, every Saturday. After you graduate from Pre-College, if you want to keep going, you audition again for acceptance into the Juilliard college.

On the day of my Pre-College audition, I went up to the third floor of the school, Room 309, where later my class had orchestra rehearsals. I sat in the lobby, waiting for Miss DeLay.

After an hour or so, she came up to me and said, "Hello, sugarplum! Come on in." Just like she was asking me into her living room.

I don't think I'd ever been more nervous. An accompanist sat at the piano, and the whole Juilliard violin jury was in the audience. Miss DeLay, fortunately (sweet, kind, wonderful woman that she is), was the first face I saw. The rest of the jury looked like this was a hanging court.

I played part of the Bruch Concerto, and a little Bach, too. When I was finished, Miss DeLay said, "Beautiful, sugarplum," and asked me to wait outside.

I left the room thinking, "God, I could have done that better, I could have done this better." I had a pretty long wait, sitting there picking at the Partridge Family stickers on my violin case.

Inside, Miss DeLay was saying she couldn't understand how I played at all using the bowings I did and holding the violin as I did. Going my own way as a student was plainly evident.

Miss DeLay saw a lot that was very bad, but also a lot that was interesting. She took me on as a student, and I was accepted into the Pre-College that same fall. Every Saturday morning, I rode in from Cherry Hill on the bus, and the other six days of the week (during my first year at Pre-College) I stayed home and practiced. To have all this time, Mama somehow arranged for me to take a whole year off from regular school—a year I'd make up for later.

From the beginning with Miss DeLay, I was trouble. I'd see kids outside her studio smoking cigarettes and telling dirty jokes. Then they'd go in to see her and be so polite, like little angels. I wanted to puke. That wasn't me.

I went in completely the opposite direction, which wasn't

such a smart thing to do either. I was very stubborn as a student, even though bad playing habits were hurting me technically.

My technique was as if I was walking with my right shoe on my left foot and my left shoe on my right foot. Even though it wasn't correct, I had been doing it so long it was comfortable. I was used to it. And I didn't want someone telling me I was doing things the wrong way.

But as my teacher, Miss DeLay was telling me to switch shoes and I didn't want to do it. It *hurt.*

An instrument requires the use of small muscles in your fingers and hands. Your body gets used to doing things in a certain way, holding an instrument a certain way, and your muscles get set. You can't just retrain your muscles on command, or so I thought.

Rather than work, I refused. I figured I got into Juilliard playing my way. I was like Rocky Balboa, another great Philadelphian. "I'm doing fine, Miss DeLay. So just teach me."

Every week I went into her studio and she'd say, "Why don't you try this fingering?"

And I'd say, "This one feels a lot better." Never mind that I couldn't get the passage and it was horribly out of tune. It felt better.

She could've just thrown me out of her class. I would have gone and that would have been the end. But she stayed with me. At the end of each lesson she'd say, "Sugarplum, you have to change that position."

I'd said, "Uh-huh."

Next week I'd do the same thing.

She'd teach me something else and at the end of the lesson she'd say, "Sugarplum . . ."

This went on for three years. Miss DeLay (who has a degree in psychology) was doing an incredibly wise thing. Unless a student is disappointed in their own playing, anything a teacher forces on them will be resisted and lost. Miss DeLay knew I had to make a decision to change on my own and she gave me the time to do it. Meanwhile, as part of the lesson, I got to listen to the other kids. Every week there was a recital.

Another student of hers would play and I'd say, "Holy cow, listen to that guy." And it slowly began to creep in; it's because they have the right position.

Miss Dorothy DeLay

If I had to sum up Miss DeLay's teaching it'd be with this: She taught me to listen to myself.

It sounds easy, but it's the hardest thing about excelling on an instrument.

As a student, you're never quite sure what to listen for in your playing. You don't have enough information. The computer in your head needs to be stocked so that when it hears the end result, it knows whether it's good or not. And if it's not good—what's wrong with it? How can it be improved?

Excelling on an instrument, building up that kind of computer, means having high goals right from the start.

A high goal when you begin playing the violin is to get through *Mary Had a Little Lamb*. Your next goal might be to have a beautiful sound, perfect intonation in musical phrasing.

When you get into the pursuit of excellence, you begin to listen for all the intricate things that make playing so vast.

If, for example, I play a passage that has a finger shift in the middle, I don't want that shift to be heard.

Unless your ears are trained, you won't hear yourself shift, though the audience may. You don't know how to hear yourself. You don't know what to listen for.

That's what Miss DeLay taught me.

She'd ask in class, "What was wrong with the passage you just played?"

Most kids would say, "Nothing" or "I don't know" or "It was fine" or "I'm not sure, something was wrong, but I'm not sure."

Miss DeLay would say, "Play it again. Really listen. What's wrong?"

"Well," someone might say, "I think the B flat is out of tune."

"Are you sure that note is out of tune? Play it again. Play it again."

"Yes, that note is out of tune."

"Why is it out of tune?"

Sometimes I'd get so mad I'd yell, "I don't know! Why are you getting paid? What is this, I'm teaching myself?"

I was right. She was teaching me to teach myself—and that's why she is a great teacher.

One of the first things you learn, from any teacher, is to learn a piece by practicing it slowly. If you're very disciplined and very determined to play a piece well, if you're going to prepare a concerto or anything that's difficult, you begin at a very slow tempo.

That's basic.

Students go to their room with a passage out of a piece and practice *diddle, iddle, iddle* while the metronome is slowly ticking. And they do it over and over again.

This is exactly what I used to do. You might think you're being very disciplined and deserve a real pat on the back. It's quite boring and requires a lot of concentration to learn a piece

Papa John, 1928.

Nanny, 1934.

Together, 1952.

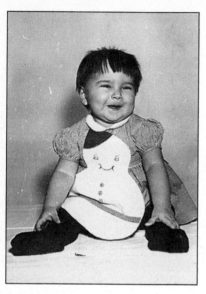

Nadja Rose, 10 1/2 months.

Three, 1964.

Four, sharing a Christmas toast
with Eric, 1965.

Five *(second from left)*, at a dance
recital, 1966.

Singing for my supper, a restaurant in Rome, 1967.

A lesson with Antonio Marchetti, 1968, (Mama looks on).

Backstage at the Robin Hood Dell, wearing my first new dress, 1971. A newspaper ran the photo caption "Pensive Prodigy." *(Philadelphia Daily News)*

Debut, the Bach A minor Concerto (first movement) with the Philadelphia Orchestra.

Rehearsing with Mama, Cherry Hill, 1973. *(Cherry Hill Courier-Post)*

With Yumi Ninomiya.

In my Curtis sweatshirt at the Académie de Musique Maurice Ravel, 1974. *(Les Medailles/St. Jean de Luz)*

Onstage, St. Jean de Luz, 1975. *Photo Velez/St. Jean de Luz.*

Papa John, Mama, Philippe Entremont, Nanny, and me in the middle, 1975, Cherry Hill.

With Cecile Licad, backstage before a recital in New Rochelle, 1976.

slowly, passage by passage. But if you're not listening to yourself, you're wasting time.

The entire passage may be very good, except for one note, and if you're not listening very carefully, you won't hear that one note.

Just as in reading music, when you practice you have to be a detective. One bad note in a passage is like an offensive line with one bad lineman. They can't pass-block, they can't run-block, their quarterback is flying into the bleachers.

Once you find that one bad note, you have to figure out why the note is bad and the others aren't.

Why?

It may be a number of reasons. For a violinist, it may mean that your left hand is going faster than your bow-arm. They may not be coordinated.

It may be that you're crossing from an A- to an E-string and the crossing isn't clear.

It may be that there's a shift in finger positions, it may be that. It may be a number of things, but you have to play detective and find out what it is.

Instead of repeatedly playing the passage for hours, it might require two minutes of listening, finding, fixing. That's it. Next passage.

Technical practice is extremely important. No matter how many musical ideas I have, if I didn't spend more than twenty years practicing, learning the craft of the violin, all those ideas wouldn't be able to come out.

As a student, from eight to twelve o'clock every morning I did exercises, scales, etudes . . . basic things that train your fingers. It's like outfielders playing catch or taking batting practice. They are the rudiments of playing that warm you up and keep your muscles in shape.

When I learned a piece, it required a different kind of practice. Now you're dealing with music, not just keeping in shape with scales or shifting patterns of vibrato.

Learning a piece can be cut down to different levels. Everybody has their own system for doing this. First, many violinists will learn the notes in a very basic, technical, rudimentary way. Just the notes, figure out the fingerings, what fingerings are good for you, figure out the bowings, and all of that.

Then you look at the piece and try to make sense of it musically. You want to understand the piece, so you analyze up and down.

You analyze it harmonically, you analyze it melodically. Then you do a technical analysis, analyzing bow patterns, bow speed—everything you do can be analyzed. That's how complicated playing the violin can be.

Basically, you're breaking a complicated piece into tiny details. Then, as you perfect each detail, you put it back together as if it were a model airplane.

The initial analysis of a piece may take months of intense work. In music, however, there's no such thing as a *final* analysis, because you'll also feel differently about a piece. You reanalyze and reanalyze the theme, the second theme, the development, how it all fits together.

A natural outcome of all this is memorization. I couldn't even say how many pieces I have committed to memory. Memorization gives some people fits, especially of large works. But fortunately it has always just come to me as I learned a piece; the result of knowing, and hearing, a piece bit by bit.

Saturdays in New York

The term "interval" refers to the scalar distance
between the two tones, measured by their
difference in pitch.

—Walter Piston

If you want to see what Juilliard Pre-College is like, walk into
the place on a Saturday. It's a madhouse. Kids running from one
class to another: Theory, Ear Training, Orchestra, and their
private lesson.

Outside of my lesson with Miss DeLay, Orchestra was my
favorite. We'd bring Lifesavers and chitchat. My friend Ellen
was in the cello section, and since the cellos and violins face each
other, we could make mouth signals back and forth. I got hol-
lered at a lot, and was suspended a few times. Once, I couldn't
come to school for three weeks because I threw a Frisbee off the
roof. Boy, was I upset.

In Ear Training class, a teacher plays two notes on the
piano. They might be two notes in succession—a melodic interval. Or two notes together—a harmonic interval. Then he asks,
"What interval is that?"

You say, "That's a minor third."

He says, "Wrong. That's a major third."

The other part of Ear Training is sight-reading.

We used a workbook by Robert Starer that featured reading exercises. You had to sing a top staff of music, the right notes, correct time, while you clapped the rhythm of notes in the lower staff. The whole class would be singing and clapping—we all hated it.

Theory class is just what it sounds like. Technical theory. Bass lines and Neapolitan sixth chords. It was very, very difficult for me. And in Juilliard, that's the way they seemed to prefer it.

In a written Ear Training test, for instance, the teacher would play intervals; you wrote down what he played; he graded it.

Now here is something I don't understand. I didn't understand it then. I don't understand it now. I will argue it with God because it's dumb.

Instead of writing M3 for a major third and m3 for a minor third, you had to use a symbol that some Juilliard genius thought up.

It looked like hieroglyphics. The perfect fifth symbol was something like three horizontal lines, two short lines in between, with a dot at the top and a little curve at the bottom.

They expected you to memorize a ton of these stupid symbols that were used only at Juilliard. At the Mannes College of Music, another New York school, they had their own geniuses and their own symbols. What's the point?

The whole reason for the class is to train your ear. Why not write P5 for a perfect fifth, and concentrate on the real task of ear training? But no. They had to complicate it with stupid symbols which I refused to learn. So I flunked the class.

Never mind that I knew what the intervals were. I used to say, "You're going to fail me because I don't know your stupid symbols, which I know for a fact are not used anywhere else outside of this building in the world of music? Fail me, go ahead!"

Then I'd go fuming in for my lesson with Miss DeLay. "Can you believe I'm failing Ear Training?"

And she'd say, "Sugarplum, sit down. Let's talk about di-
plomacy." I was always so mad that anything she said went in
one ear and right out the other.

Never in my life did I have any kind of patience with things
that weren't logical: with people who make more out of their
jobs than is there; with people who can't do their jobs so you
wind up doing it for them; with stupid little rules that society
has made up; things that make no sense but you have to accept
them.

Fortunately, Miss DeLay had patience for me.

When I started my second year of Saturdays at Pre-College
in 1976, I needed to catch up on the regular school I missed. So
for my high school education, I was enrolled in what's called an
alternative private school. It was the Penn Center Academy, on
Arch Street in Philly, a school that had an accelerated program.

"Accelerated" doesn't mean Penn Center was a school for
geniuses. The idea was just to finish two years in one, one year
per semester. For most of the students, if they finished school at
all, it was going to have to be quick.

Penn Center did have some very good teachers; inspiring
teachers for subjects that never inspired me before, especially
literature and writing. I even came to understand what *Macbeth*
was about. But the place was a typical tough inner-city school.

I met a girl there named Nigel who quickly became my
friend. She was fourteen and had already had two abortions and
been arrested for possession of drugs.

I, on the other hand, was a nerd among sharks.

Nigel

"It's a time for joy, a time for tears;
A time we'll treasure through the years.
We'll remember always . . . Graduation day."

—Joe and Noel Sherman

I was a very skinny, runty kid at fifteen; braces, wire-rimmed granny glasses, my hair was pulled back in a long plait.

The boys basically ignored me. A little cursing, but that was all.

But the girls in Penn Center . . .

Anyone who sticks out in high school is bound to get hammered down. It's some kind of tribal law that kids agree to follow. Since Nigel and I were loners, we were the nails.

The worst of it came after school. Every day, I turned the corner, and sure enough, there were eight girls standing there.

They wouldn't let you pass. They'd knock the stuff out of your hands, taunt you, and then the kicking and punching would start.

I am not a crybaby. I hardly ever cried since my lessons with Ferras. But I'd go home crying every day.

Nigel always fought back, but I was too overwhelmed to do anything except take the racking. Growing up and being in school is so difficult already—who needs that kind of crap?

And then I won the Philly Orchestra prize for the third time, and it was in the newspaper along with my picture. Word got around: I was worse than a nerd. I was a nerd who played the violin.

I did my best to stay away from them that day. But every once in a while, I'd look up during the class and see them staring at me.

Dead meat, they'd say. *You're dead. After school, you wait.*

Fear has a taste, and the taste got worse and worse as the day went by. I finally saw Nigel at lunch.

"You have to fight back," she said.

"I don't know how to fight them."

"Just get in the first punch," Nigel said. "Hit them first and run like hell."

Right then, a group was walking over to us. They weren't after signatures in their yearbooks. From the looks of things, their fun was going to start a little early.

"Like this." Nigel swung and doubled over the nearest girl. We took off and ran like crazy.

God only knows why, but nothing else happened until the last school bell. I hung around my locker as long as I could. An empty school is creepy. Staying inside wasn't making me feel any better.

I took my books and slowly started walking down the steps. Down the steps, on to the sidewalk, and . . .

"Look who's here," a voice beside me said. I tensed to jump and run when from the other side something hard hit the back of my neck.

My books fell, and I stumbled. Someone kicked my knee, someone else pushed me from behind. This wasn't *fair*.

I got my balance, wheeled around, and hit the first face I saw. I'm not too sure what happened next. There was shouting, cursing, hitting, until I ran. I ran and I ran. I had lost my books, so at least there was no homework that night.

I was bruised, scraped, and sore all over. But the next day

in school, I was pleased to see I had managed to bruise a few of them myself.

Things were easier after that, but fighting back wasn't the only reason. I wasn't required to take gym until the second semester. I had been athletic ever since I was little; the other girls just weren't. No matter what we were doing—volleyball, swimming, basketball—I came to be the first choice because I was always determined to do the best I could. The other girls began to accept me. Either that, or as time went by, they just got bored beating me up.

In Phys. Ed., I met a wonderful coach. He encouraged me to be a runner. He thought I'd make a good sprinter; maybe he'd seen me race for the Jersey bus every day.

So I tried it and found that I loved it. There's something wonderful about pushing yourself, stretching yourself, going flat out and finding an extra reserve that you never knew was there.

I would get up an hour early, at five in the morning, and run before I had to practice. And I would run after school too. I dreamed of running in the Olympics: *Another gold medal for "Flash" Salerno-Sonnenberg!*

That particular bubble burst when Mama finally said, "You know, you're going to have to choose because you're spending too much time running. Are you going to run or are you going to play the violin?"

I told her I'd think about it overnight. I took it very seriously. Little did I know I didn't have a choice. My mother just made it seem that way.

I thought it over and in the morning I said, "I want to play the violin."

She said, "Fine. I accept that choice."

Much later Mama told me, "You know, if you had chosen to run, I would have said, Forget it!"

I told the coach I had to quit. Going for the gold just wasn't in the cards. Now I run for planes, and that's it.

There were two graduations that spring when I was seventeen. I graduated from Penn Center, and from Pre-College (and soon after passed the Juilliard School of Music audition).

For years, my mother always told me, "Nadja, when you

graduate from high school it will be the saddest day of your life. Those are going to be beautiful years. When I graduated from high school, I cried for weeks because you never can go back."

No way.

When the last bell rang on graduation day, I was down the stairs of Penn Center two steps at a time. Why should I be sorry to leave that behind? I was walking on air. It wasn't until later that I did miss something. I never saw Nigel again.

Crisis

Music is so enormous that unless you know what you are doing and why, it can envelop you in a state of perpetual anxiety and torture.

—Maria Callas

Back when my mother first put the violin under my chin, I didn't just accept it because I was a wimp. As you probably know by now, I never listened to authority easily.

I fought my mother and I fought my teachers a lot. But I did listen to logic easily. Why would Mama want me to play the violin if it were bad for me? I trusted her love, so playing the violin must be good.

Maybe I wasn't the kid who was Mr. Spock, but that's logical enough for me.

I never questioned why I was playing the violin. At the age of twelve I wasn't thinking about my life. At the age of sixteen I cared about the Yankees. I was falling in love and wondering what I should do with my hair.

A life as a musician didn't seem particularly noble at that age, but playing violin was something I could do, so I did it. The older I got, the better I got. And the better I got, the harder it would be to quit and become something useful.

During my first year of college at Juilliard, I resolved to work out my technical problems with Miss DeLay. I just took it for granted that I would keep getting better. I never thought I might reach the limit of my talent, or end up not good enough to make it.

But I began to see that I hadn't even begun to work. There were college players my age and younger who could blow me out of the room. All of them were intensely ambitious about making a career and I finally realized a career is what I wanted too. At the same time, though, I began to feel I'd come to that realization too late.

As this was hitting me, I was seventeen and living alone in New York City. New York isn't a great place to be broke. Or depressed. I had just ended a relationship, so I was lovelorn, miserable, and full of self-doubt. The only place I could be happy was in an orchestra.

Classical music is immersed in tradition. Tradition is wonderful, but it can also be very damaging. Women, for example, are often expected to be "feminine" in their playing, more demure than men. When people are expected to act a certain way throughout the ages, no matter what else has changed, I think it's not so smart. And classical music suffers from it.

But there are certain traditions in classical music that are wonderful and should stay. The oboe, for instance, gives the A to tune the orchestra. It's done that way in the United States, in Iron Curtain countries, in Finland, in Africa; that's the way it is.

I have no idea why it started. Why the oboe and not the clarinet? I don't know. It's just a sweet tradition, one thing you can always count on.

Orchestra at Juilliard was required. It lasted three hours with one fifteen-minute break. As soon as we got into the hall it was:

"Oh my God, he asked me out . . ."

"Did you see who she was speaking to . . . ?"

"Can I have some of that Twinkie?"

"Did you call him last night?"

"What happened. . . ?"

Then back to Orchestra.

No matter how bad my mental health got, the string section was always there to cheer me up; the music too, of course, except during contemporary week. I'm such a fan of melody that unfortunately not all contemporary music is for me.

Outside of Juilliard, orchestras were a place to earn rent and food money. I joined a ballet orchestra and it led to a glimpse of a world I could only admire from the outside.

A high point came when Natalia Makarova needed a soloist for a pas de deux with Anthony Dowell. The ballet was to a Bach sonata for violin and harpsichord, and I got the job.

I was thrust into the world of ballet, in rehearsals with Makarova, and I loved it. Since then, I've occasionally performed with ballet companies. It's the closest I'll ever come to being part of the ballet.

Despite anything positive happening around me though, the big question wouldn't go away. Would I be good enough to make it? Could I make a living as a violinist? The more I thought about it, the worse things got.

A piece such as the *Carmen Fantasy* (a violin transcription of Bizet's opera by Sarasate) is very hard technically. I played it easily when I didn't know how hard it was. Then I turned eighteen and thought, "My God, that piece is really difficult! How did I ever play it?"

And as I realized it was hard, I couldn't play it at all. Never mind that I played it just fine yesterday.

I started realizing how difficult it was to play thirds. The lower my self-confidence sunk, the more I thought, "How did I ever do any of this before?"

By the time I was halfway through being nineteen, I couldn't play a G major scale in tune. I was a cripple on the instrument. It got to the point where I didn't even want to hear myself play because I sounded so bad. It was torture. I stopped playing the violin for seven long months: the worst period of my life.

I was used to success, to the prodigy label in newspapers, and now I felt like a failure. A has-been. I couldn't play anymore, and my life was over. I felt like a bum, that I should go hang out on the Bowery.

I started showing up for my lesson without my fiddle. Thank God, Miss DeLay understood, and we spent the lesson time talking about music, life, and my problems.

Everything I was going through boiled down to fear. Fear of trying and failing. To measure up against all those wonderfully talented players at Juilliard, I would have to commit myself as never before. And if I disciplined myself to really work, and gave the violin my all, and *failed* . . . I would have to deal with it forever.

If you go to an audition and don't really try, if you're not really prepared, if you didn't work as hard as you could have and you don't win, you have an excuse.

"Honest," you can say, "if I had worked harder, I would have won." But nothing is harder than saying, "I gave it my all and it wasn't good enough."

Even having nothing to do with music, that's a really hard thing for anybody to face. It's very hard to give everything you have and then hear someone say, "Sorry. Do something else."

I had to face that as a little kid in ballet class. There was a time when I'd have given anything to float like a leaf in a tutu. But there was just no way I was ever meant to dance. No way on earth I could be that graceful, even if Baryshnikov was coaching me every day.

Ballerinas come out onstage and even the way they bow— oh, please—it's amazing. They have a highly developed sense of expressing themselves through their body. It's like their brains are linked directly to their arms and legs. Did you ever hear a ballerina speak?

Not long after I turned twenty, one week, like every week, I went to see Miss DeLay.

This time, Miss DeLay looked at me and said, "Listen, If you don't bring your violin next week, I'm throwing you out of my class."

And I laughed. I thought she and I were such good friends, she would never do that.

Miss DeLay rose from the couch and, in a very calm way,

said, "I'm not kidding. If you're going to waste your talent, I don't want to be part of it. This has gone on long enough."

Then she walked out of the room.

I went home in deep shock. I was petrified. Should I quit? Could I lose Miss DeLay as a teacher and friend? There was one person I could talk to, my oldest friend, Cecile Licad.

Cecile had stayed at Curtis after I left and then moved on to the Institute for Young Musicians in Vermont. But we had stayed best buddies and, over the years, had played many recitals together—from New Rochelle to Manila. Thankfully, Cecile was living nearby in New York just then and I called her immediately.

"Cecile," I said, "what am I going to do?"

Cecile hardly ever speaks, but when she does it's usually wise for you to listen.

There was a pause, and then she said in her wonderful gruff voice, "Don't give up."

Three words. That was it.

"Okay, Cecile. I won't."

Now I just needed to prove it.

The 1981 Walter W. Naumburg International Violin Competition was coming up in two months. I was in no shape for a competition. I hadn't touched the violin for more than half a year. I had no idea if I could touch the violin now without feeling sick. If I could even manage to get into the finals of the competition, it would be a miracle.

The winner would receive three thousand dollars and solo recitals at the Library of Congress, Lincoln Center's Alice Tully Hall, and the Ambassador Auditorium in Pasadena. There would also be performances with the Chicago Symphony, the American Symphony Orchestra in Carnegie Hall, and with orchestras in Detroit, Buffalo, Aspen, and Los Angeles.

I put my name down for the audition.

Despite all the fear, all the self-doubt, I needed to take a shot. I needed to see what I was made of.

I wanted to live. Even as an honest failure.

Miss Dorothy DeLay. *Charles Abbott*

An Itzhak Perlman
master class,
Aspen, 1979.
Charles Abbott

Being coached by Dorothy DeLay, 1980, *(Also opposite page).*
Charles Abbott

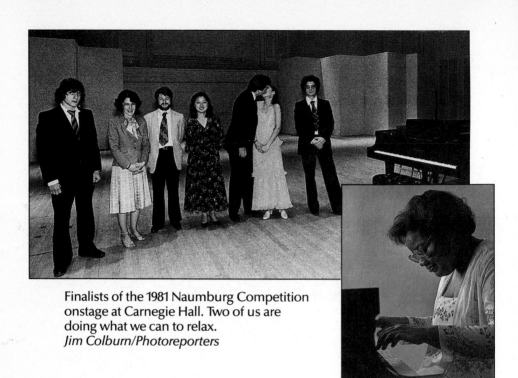

Finalists of the 1981 Naumburg Competition
onstage at Carnegie Hall. Two of us are
doing what we can to relax.
Jim Colburn/Photoreporters

Sandra Rivers. *Peter Schaaf*

Debut with the Chicago Symphony, 1981; Kurt Masur conducts.

Aspen Music Festival, 1984. *Charles Abbott*

In back of the string section: a gathering of Miss DeLay's students play a Kreutzer exercise at her seventieth birthday party, 1987. *Peter Schaaf*

Ravinia, 1987,
a rehearsal
with James Levine.

A soloist's bow: with Peter Martins and Kate Johnson, New York City
Ballet, 1988. *Paul Kolnik*

Listening to a playback with Gerard Schwarz. *Don Hunstein*

In the studio with Cecile Licad, 1988. *Daniel Root*

With Miss DeLay. *Charles Abbott*

Naumburg

The majority of those who wish to become musicians have
no idea of the difficulties they will have to surmount,
the moral tortures they will be called upon to endure,
the disillusions they will experience,
before they win recognition.

—Leopold Auer

From the day I signed up for the Naumburg Competition,
everything changed. I had made a decision to start again, to save
my life, and that meant a 360-degree turnaround.

I immersed myself in practicing. An enormous amount of
work had to be done in two months. I went from not practicing
at all to thirteen hours a day.

My fingers were like linguine. I spent two weeks just playing
scales. If I thought I sounded bad before, now I sounded worse
than awful.

At the time I lived on 72nd Street, close to West End Avenue. I had an efficiency apartment with a window the size of a
shoebox. I didn't do my laundry, I left my apartment only to
walk to Juilliard—and not on Broadway like everyone else. I
walked up Amsterdam Avenue because I didn't want to see any-

body, didn't want to bump into anybody, didn't want anyone to ask what I was doing.

I stopped going to classes and became a hermit. I even talked Miss DeLay into giving my lesson at night.

My eating habits were awful. I lived on fried sausages, a pint of peanut butter/chocolate ice cream, and a gallon of Coca-Cola every day. That's all I ate for eight weeks.

I was nuts. I was completely obsessed with getting back into shape, with doing well in this competition. If I could, people would know I was still on earth. Not to count me out; to stop asking, "Whatever happened to Nadja?"

The last week before the Naumburg auditions, I couldn't touch the violin. I had worked and worked and worked and worked and then I just couldn't work anymore.

I certainly could have used it. I wasn't as prepared as I should have been. But I simply had to say, "Nadja, you've dedicated yourself to this thing. Ready or not, do your best."

Fifty violinists from around the world auditioned for the competition on May 25, 26, and 27, 1981. Those that made it past the preliminaries would go on to the semifinals. Those that passed that stage would go to the finals. In years past, one violinist was chosen as winner and two received second and third place.

On May 26, the day of my audition, I went to the Merkin Concert Hall at 67th Street and Broadway. I waited, played for twenty minutes, and went home. I couldn't tell whether the preliminary judges were impressed or not. I'd find out the next evening.

Maybe subconsciously I was trying to keep busy; that night, when I fried the sausages, I accidentally set my apartment on fire. I grabbed my cat and my violin, and ran out the door. The fire was put out, but everything in my place was wrecked.

Fortunately, the phone was okay and on the evening of May 27, I had the news from Lucy Rowan Mann of Naumburg. Thirteen of us had made it.

Talk about mixed emotions. I was thrilled to be among the thirteen; a group that included established violinists, some of whom had already made records. But it also meant I had to play the next day in the semifinals of the competition.

Everyone entering the competition had been given two lists of concertos. One was a list of standard repertory pieces. The other list was twentieth-century repertory. For our big competition piece, we were to choose from each list and play a movement from one in the semifinals, and a movement from the other in the finals—if we made it that far.

From the standard repertory list, I chose the Tchaikovsky Concerto. I had been playing the Tchaik for three years, so it was a good piece for me.

From the twentieth-century list, I chose the Prokofiev G minor Concerto. I had never played it onstage before.

My goal had been just passing the auditions, but now my thought pattern began to change. If I wanted a sliver of a chance of advancing again, my brain said, "Play your strong piece first."

Logically, I should play the Tchaikovsky in the semifinals just to make it to the next stage. Who cared if that left me with a piece I probably wouldn't play as well in the finals of the competition? It'd be a miracle to get that far.

There wouldn't be more than seven violinists chosen for the final round, and if I were in the top seven of an international group, that was plenty good enough.

The semifinals were held on May 28 in Merkin Concert Hall. You were to play for thirty minutes: your big piece first, then the judges would ask to hear another.

There was a panel of eight judges. They had a piece of paper with my choices of the Tchaikovsky and the Prokofiev in front of them. "Which would you like to play?" the asked.

I said meekly, "Prokofiev."

My brain and all the logic in the world had said play your strong piece. My heart said, "Go for it all. Play your weak piece now, save Tchaikovsky for the finals."

Maybe I don't listen to logic so easily after all.

My good friend, the pianist Sandra Rivers, had been chosen as accompanist for the competition. She knew I was nervous. There had been a very short time to prepare; I was sure there'd be memory slips, that I'd blank out in the middle and the judges would throw me out. My hands were like ice.

The first eight measures of the Prokofiev don't have accompaniment. The violin starts the piece alone. So I started playing.

I got through the first movement and Sandra said later my face was white as snow. She said I was so tense, I was beyond shaking. Just a solid brick.

It was the best I'd ever played it. No memory slips at all. Technically, musically, it was there.

I finished it thinking, "Have I sold my soul for this? Is the devil going to visit me at midnight? How come it went so well?"

I didn't know why, but often I do my best under the worst of circumstances. I don't know if it's guts or a determination not to disappoint people. Who knows what it is, but it came through for me, and I thank God for that.

As the first movement ended, the judges said, "Thank you." Then they asked for the *Carmen Fantasy*.

I turned and asked Sandy for an A, to retune, and later she said the blood was just rushing back into my face.

I whispered, "Sandy, I made it. I did it."

"Yeah," she whispered back, kiddingly, "too bad you didn't screw up. Maybe next time."

At that point I didn't care if I did make the finals because I had played the Prokofiev so well. I was so proud of myself for coming through.

I needed a shot in the arm; that afternoon I got evicted. While I was at Merkin, my moped had blown up. For my landlord, that was the last straw.

What good news. I was completely broke and didn't have the next month's rent anyway. The landlord wanted me out that day. I said, "Please, can I have two days? I might get into the finals, can I please go through this first?"

I talked him into it, and got back to my place in time for the phone call. "Congratulations, Nadja," they said. "You have made the finals."

I had achieved the ridiculously unlikely, and I had saved my best piece. Yet part of me was sorry. I wanted it to be over already. In the three days from the preliminaries to the semi-finals, I lost eight pounds. I was so tired of the pressure.

There was a fellow who advanced to the finals with me, an old, good friend since Pre-College. Competition against friends is inevitable in music, but I never saw competition push a friendship out the window so quickly. By the day of the finals, I hated him and he hated me. Pressure was that intense.

The finals were held on May 29 at Carnegie Hall and open to the public. I was the fourth violinist of the morning, then there was a lunch break, and three more violinists in the afternoon.

I played my Tchaikovsky, Saint-Saëns's *Havanaise,* and Ravel's *Tzigane* for the judges: managers, famous violinists, teachers, and critics. I went on stage at five past eleven and finished at noon. Those fifty-five minutes seemed like three days.

I was so relieved when I finished playing; I was finished! It's impossible to say how happy I was to see the dressing room. I destroyed my gown tearing it off, changed, and went out for lunch with my friends.

It was like coming back from the grave. We laughed and joked and I got caught up on *General Hospital.* I was calm but thrilled it was over. I made it to the finals, that's it, I'm done.

As I returned to Carnegie Hall to hear the other violinists, I realized I'd made a big mistake: they might ask for recalls. A recall is when they can't decide between two people and they want you to play again. It's been done; it's done all the time in competitions. No way was I in shape to go onstage and play again.

In the late afternoon, the competition was over. Everybody had finished playing. Quite luckily—no recalls.

The judges deliberated for an hour. The tension in the air was unbelievable. All the violinists were sitting with their little circle of friends. I had my few friends around me, but no one was saying much now.

Finally, the Naumburg Foundation president—founder and first violinist of the Juilliard String Quartet and that year's presenter—Robert Mann came on stage.

"It's always so difficult to choose . . . " he began.

The Prize

Every year we hold this competition," Robert Mann said. "And in the past, we've awarded three prizes. This year we've elected to only have one prize, the first prize."

My heart sank. Nothing for me. Not even Miss Congeniality.

"We have found," Mann went on, "that second place usually brings great dismay to the artist because they feel like a loser. We don't want anyone here to feel like a loser. Every finalist will receive five hundred dollars except the winner, who will receive three thousand dollars."

And then he repeated how difficult it was to choose, how well everyone had played . . . dah, dah, dah.

I was looking down at the floor.

"The winner is . . ."

And he said my name.

A friend next to me said, "Nadja, I think you won!"

I went numb. My friends pulled me up and pointed me toward the stage. It was a long walk because I had slipped into a seat in the back.

Sitting up in front was my old friend. I would have to walk right past him and I was dreading it, but before I could, he got up and stopped me.

He threw his arms around me and I threw my arms around him. I kept telling him how sorry I was. I was holding him and started to cry, saying, "I'm sorry, I'm sorry, I'm sorry." I didn't want to lose, but I really didn't want him to lose either. And he was holding me and saying, "Don't be sorry. I'm so proud of you." It was over, and we would be friends again.

I took my bow, then ran to Juilliard. Ten blocks uptown, one block west, to give Miss DeLay the news. She could be proud of me now, too.

Suddenly, everything was clear. Playing the violin is what I'd do with my life. Heaven handed me a prize: "You've been through a lot, kid. Here's an international competition."

Everything had changed when I prepared for the Naumburg, and now everything changed again. I bought a gown at Saks that cost as much as a season ticket at Yankee Stadium (I kept thinking I could find something as good for five dollars at a garage sale). I made my first recording—Fauré and Prokofiev sonatas with Sandra Rivers on the Musicmasters label. Between September 1981 and May 1982, I played a hundred concerts in America, made one trip to Europe, then two months of summer festivals. And people asked me back.

There was a great deal of anxiety playing in Europe for the first time. American musicians have their nationality to overcome. When you play Beethoven in Germany, no matter what, they're going to hate you. The audience has come to hear the American violinist who dares to play Beethoven.

My first time in Germany, walking onstage and feeling the vibes, I would rather have been a fire hydrant on Broadway. But I was able to rely on my self-confidence to pull me through.

Self-confidence onstage doesn't mean a lack of nerves backstage. The stakes had increased. This wasn't practice anymore, this was my life. I'd stare into a dressing-room mirror and say, "Nadja, people have bought tickets, hired baby-sitters, you've got to calm down; go out there and prove yourself."

Every night I'd prove myself again. My life work had truly begun.

Solo

Music is my mistress, and she plays second fiddle
to no one.

—Duke Ellington

ot every change after winning the Naumburg was so good.
It's amazing how sometimes just when you've won a major
battle on the inside, something catastrophic will happen on the
outside. During all this success and inner triumph for me, both
my grandparents died of cancer, just one year apart.

Nanny's death deeply affected my family. She was our Scar-
lett O'Hara. All the relatives revolved around her, gathering
their vitality from her and their unifying sense of tradition. Her
passing was more than we could endure.

Within another twelve months the whole family fell apart.
Unity ended. I was in New York City, my mother was in New
Jersey, God knows where my brother was. Aunts, uncles, cous-
ins seemed to scatter to the four winds. I learned that one does

not always have to be an orphan to be orphaned by circumstances.

It was at this time that I came to rely on friendship for a family's support, warmth, and caring. Necessity compelled me to create my own family of friends. This is never a replacement for the real thing, if you're lucky enough to have a family intact, but it's the next best thing if you're not.

Friends—and I mean true friends—reserve nothing: the property of one belongs to the other. Call it mutual adoption, call it a necessity of life. Anyway you put it, I'm grateful for my friends and always will be.

And I was ecstatic about news from Cecile Licad.

Nineteen eighty-one was her year of recognition as well. The year before she had made her professional debut at the Tanglewood Festival, and in '81 Cecile was the first pianist in ten years to receive the Gold Medal from the Leventritt Foundation.

The Leventritt Gold Medal isn't based on a competition; it's awarded by a panel of musicians who follow a young musician's career over a period of time. As part of the award, Cecile played a concert that October with Zubin Mehta and the New York Philharmonic.

Another of my old bonds was broken when I left Juilliard a year after Naumburg. I was out of town playing so much that I was failing every course. Beside, school was never the place I learned most. Other people love it. There are people in Juilliard now who were there when I arrived in Pre-College. They have gray hair now, these professional students.

I always believed that along with studying, practicing, and musical analysis, the rest of the day is just as important to my playing.

Many music students at a place such as Juilliard stay in practice rooms all day. There are no windows, no air. And when it comes to performance, they often approach it as if they were still in their room.

Music is an emotional business. I have to pour out my soul every time I play. I'm not going to have much to pour out if I sit in a room all day long. From eight to twelve, I'm going to learn about the violin. The rest of the day, I'm going to learn about music.

Not many people I know agree with me, but I think by going to the ballet or to the museum or even by seeing bums on the street, I'm going to learn about music, I'm going to learn about performance. I'm going to learn about stage presence from watching a dancer. You might not guess that from seeing me, but it's true.

Music is *do* to *do*. Seven notes.

The amazing thing is that it's what you do with those seven notes as a composer, the order in which they're written, the harmonies you create, the rhythm in which they're played, that makes you a genius or a failure.

And it's how you play those seven notes that qualifies you as an artist or not.

I go to Yankee Stadium and hear the organ playing and see the crowd react to the music—all of it goes into one thing, which is how I play music on stage.

Listening to pop artists, same thing; listening to Al Jarreau or Miles Davis improvise can teach you a lot. Miles Davis, in fact, was a trumpet player at Juilliard who really got his education at 52nd Street jazz clubs.

Classical musicians improvise with phrasing, but not with the music itself as jazz musicians do. We're honor-bound not to change the notes. We have to play what Mendelssohn and Tchaikovsky wrote, what's on the page, otherwise we're desecrating their music.

Yet if we all play those notes in exactly the same dynamic with exactly the same tempo, exactly the same phrasing with exactly the same fingerings and bowings—why have a thousand violinists in the world? Why not just one? Why not a computer, or just the same old recordings?

What separates all of us is how we approach those notes.

I approach them as I do with everything that is inside me. I do not change as a person when I'm onstage as if I'm a reserved musician now and I'm going to play this piece as I was taught to play it.

The Zone is my ideal. It's a word I use to describe a certain feeling onstage, a feeling that everything is right. You've reached the Zone when everybody in the audience is responding to what you're saying and you aren't battling yourself. All the technical work and what you want to say have come together. It's what I've spent my life trying to achieve. Nothing can go wrong when you've reached the Zone.

Critics do get their say, though, and some, especially early in my career, took me to task for things outside the music. Some critics have said (in various ways) that I act more like an athlete on stage than a proper classical musician. All right, I'll take that as a compliment.

On the diamond, a batter hits a long drive to right center and the outfielder goes back, back, back, back . . . and leaps. He jumps that extra inch and catches the ball just as it's about to go into the stands. The crowd goes crazy; he stopped a home run.

Violinists know what that extra effort is like.

Say the most difficult part in a concerto is coming up. It's really hard and right after it comes a big *tutti fortissimo*—the whole orchestra playing very loud.

Now, as a violinist you know that you're either going to capture that big moment or you're going to blow it. If you're careful, you'll approach that difficult passage conservatively and you'll get it. It won't be exciting, but the orchestra will come in and it'll be over.

But if you really go for it, take a chance and not be conservative, it could be fantastic. You're going to get an incredible feeling of elation if you get it. And if you don't, you tried. That's my approach. I would never be careful at that moment.

The time to be careful is when you prepare. All the eight-to-twelve work on technique, all the physical training and mental analysis, are inside waiting to be used. The same is true for what I've learned after practice.

When you keep your eyes and ears open, experiences are constantly building up inside your body. They stay there to be tapped when you need them, whatever your work happens to be.

Mine is playing the violin. And reaching for the Zone.

Coda

Sometimes I feel I worked so hard for what I have yet am only beginning to work. No matter how much you do for the craft of your instrument, and the beauty of music, you're still a lucky son of a gun to concertize and make records.

Some people, even people who might become quite good at an instrument, were just not born for the business of music. Making music for a living, being a soloist, traveling, having a career—that's the business of music. Why is the business so hard?

First of all, there aren't many things that take more time than learning an instrument.

An actor will memorize his lines, and if he has any semblance of personality, he can usually find his way through a part. If you don't believe me, stay home and watch the soaps some afternoon.

You can't fake the Bruch Concerto if you can't play the violin. It takes many years to play something that complex. If you started the violin today, it might take you fifteen years to do it. And while you're conquering *Czardas*, there are twelve-year-olds whipping through Bruch as if it was *Zippety-Do-Dah*.

This isn't to say that an early start will guarantee success any more than a late start will guarantee failure. It's possible that someone who's never touched an instrument has the most incredible musical mind the world will ever know. You should never say, "I'm already too old to start playing." So you might not make a debut until you're older—so what?

If your genius is obvious, and your debut is outlandishly wonderful, then you'll go right to the top no matter how old or young you are.

The musical community is very small, especially the classical music community. I could play a concert in Dubuque and a conductor may hear me who happens to have a small orchestra in Frankfurt. He'll go back to Germany and before I know it, I'll be invited there because he liked the way I played.

News of a debut that's outrageous, that people flipped over, will travel throughout the entire classical music community within two weeks no matter where the debut took place. Word of mouth is that quick.

So time learning an instrument isn't the only factor in the business of music. The most important, mysterious, and sometimes heartbreaking thing is having a talent that people will appreciate. If you have that talent, and you have determination to succeed, you're more than halfway to the goal.

Competitions are one way of testing appreciation. If you win, you get a lot of recognition overnight. But a competition will only give you initial debuts in various cities. Winning a competition, and initial debuts, do not mean success. You have one chance in a city. If they like you, they'll rebook you. That's business. And it's the rebookings, reengagements, that mean a career.

You could have a résumé that's one word long, but if an audience went nuts for you, stood up and cheered, if the conductor liked you, the orchestra liked you, the orchestra manager liked you, the guy backstage opening the door liked you—you'll be invited back.

You could also have won every competition on earth, but if everybody falls asleep . . . forget it. You won't be asked back.

There are definitely ways to make a first-class career without winning a competition. There are lots of people who have won very prestigious awards and are going nowhere slowly.

I'm a true believer in the heart winning out. If your spirit is there and if your talent is that great, it will win out. It will win someday. You may have to wait for it to happen, but it will happen.

I'll give an example. There's a pianist named Ivo Pogorelich. He entered the Chopin International Competition, a very big competition in Warsaw. The judges were a panel of pianists, including Martha Argerich. She was the only judge who loved his playing. The others hated it because Pogorelich's Chopin is really different and quite challenging.

Argerich protested the other judges' decision against him so heatedly that she finally removed herself from the panel. Pogorelich won second prize and another pianist that no one's ever heard of, and no one ever will, won the grand prize.

So it often doesn't matter. There have been guys who've won the Van Cliburn Competition, the Naumburg, the Queen Elizabeth, and that may be the peak of their career. You can get initial concerts, but if no one's interested in your style of playing, you'll have that two or three years of work and that's it.

One more thing goes into building a career: luck. I've heard festival organizers say, "We had a blond violinist last year. This year we'll get a brunette one." The classical music field is not devoid of that kind of nonsense. A certain amount of luck is involved in anyone's career.

Of course, a lot of people drop out before they even get to career stage.

When you start playing an instrument when you're five or eight, it's easy to get smitten with this new thing, this new toy. It makes noise and you think, Maybe I can play this piece and maybe I can get good enough to play that piece.

Then three months later, you think, Naw, never mind.

That's very, very common.

Or you work and work and work and still you see that other players are better than you. Then you realize, as happened to me, that you have to work even harder, and you begin to realize how difficult it is to play well. And that's scary.

There's also outside pressure. In Juilliard, I saw so many kids, more often than not, whose parents were at best supportive but wished their kids would get a real job someday.

Fortunately, making music and being a violinist was never something to be ashamed of in my family. But parents, generally, would rather their kids study to be doctors and lawyers. Music isn't an easy life; very few musicians actually make it and have comfortable lives.

You should know, though, that a career as a player isn't the only way to have a life in music.

When you go to a concert, you see the performers onstage, or the orchestra in the pit, and you see the conductor come out and wave his arms and the concert's over. That's what you see. But there are people directly involved in music behind the scenes that you don't see.

No performer can do without a manager. Managers are people who need to know music. They get you concerts, they book you, they represent you. It's impossible not to have one.

Performing artists need someone to handle publicity so there's a chance people will hear you're in town. Publicity agents need to know music. How could they represent someone if they didn't? Is a performer good? What makes them special?

Many publicity agents, like managers, were musicians who reached the point where playing just wasn't a necessity anymore. The same can be said of some photographers, critics, writers, music copyists, people in radio, recording, publishing, and people on the organizational side. If you want to put together a festival, or produce a concert series—you have to know music. All the people backstage, the ones you don't see, have to know music.

The thing all these people have in common is that a life in music is a calling. If you want that life, in one way or another, you can have it.

But you also must be willing to accept the price.

There's no way that being a traveling artist, that getting on a plane, is good for you. The air, the food difference, the time difference when you land, the weather—constant travel isn't good for anyone. Sometimes I feel like airline food that's been through the microwave four times.

I've played concerts with a 102 temperature and bronchitis. If something goes wrong personally, I don't have the luxury of sitting down and being depressed because I have to be at the airport.

It's hard to maintain relationships when you're constantly going somewhere. Still, I'm glad to say, my family of friends keeps growing. Cecile Licad married the cellist Antonio Meneses, and I'm the proud godmother of their child. Cecile and I recorded a sonata album in 1988; we still play concerts together from time to time, and we're still closest friends. It's a wonderful change to have such good company on the road.

Generally, the life-style of a concert artist is no good at all, but the playing makes up for it. Every violinist can't play in one city, so we have to travel. It's something I have to accept because there is a choice. I don't have to play the violin. I don't have to go around the world making music. But if I want to do that, if I want to be a soloist, then it's something that comes with the territory. So is sorting out arguments between heart and brain.

I may want to go to a particular city and play a piece I love. Instinctively and emotionally, I want to play a piece. But my brain says the audience may not be ready for this piece. The orchestra may not be ready for this piece.

If the conductor doesn't want to play it, you may not be invited back if you insist. That's the brain talking, the business of music.

Then there's the heart, the music itself speaking: I love this piece and I want to play it.

There have been a lot of split decisions.

Early in my career, I got a lot of flak for programming what the critics called audience-response pieces, otherwise known as show pieces—pieces such as the Saint-Saëns *Introduction and Rondo* and the *Carmen Fantasy*. I used to play them at the end of a concert. After you've done a lot of serious work, it's nice to end like Errol Flynn.

I cut them from my program after a while because I didn't want to deal with criticism in the papers. You have to be careful to program serious music in big cities. God forbid you should play Fritz Kreisler in New York! If you do, you're cheap, you're nothing. Kreisler is beautiful. Fine. I'll play him for myself.

Fortunately, there's one way to reach listeners without travel. When I record, the most difficult thing is not to let the permanence of what I'm doing cloud my instinctive way of making music.

For anyone, the initial struggle in the recording studio is to forget that there are mikes and tape is rolling. Play the way you play, your personality. Don't hide your personality because you want the piece to be technically perfect.

Unlike a live performance, there is a chance for a Take 2, but you can't be lulled into carelessness either. You can't think, "Hey, I didn't get it today, I'll get it tomorrow."

No. You're in a time slot and you have to finish a recording within three hours. And that is very much on an artist's mind. Everybody in the studio is being paid, a record has a budget, time is money.

Say you have three hours to record a thirty-minute piece. Think that's a lot of time? It's not. The first thing you do in the studio is a sound check on the mikes. Then you have rehearsal. Before you even start recording, an hour has gone by at the very least.

Then you play the thirty-minute piece and listen as it's played back. That cuts your time in half, listening to see what it needs.

You don't actually have three hours to record a thirty-minute piece. At best, you have an hour and twenty minutes. That gives you two takes, maybe three takes here and there on difficult spots.

Unfortunately, that's the business and you have to work around it. There's a lot you simply have to accept.

Not that I'm complaining. I have nothing to complain

about. Sometimes it's a little frightening to get what you work for. But I wouldn't trade places with anyone.

If you play concerts, teach, and make recordings, that's all a musician can expect, and I do all three. Now life is a matter of finding a greater balance and, of course, always becoming a better player.

Balance is so very difficult to achieve. It means finding time and peace and quiet to sit down and evaluate things, to snap back to center if you've leaned too far in any one direction. That's hard when there's so much to strive for, so much to know, so much work to be done.

Perhaps the thoughts and feelings I've shared in this book could lead you to believe a serious life in music is hardly worth the trouble. I can honestly tell you that nothing could be less accurate.

Once, at a post-concert reception, a surgeon stated in a mildly condescending way that *his* occupation was more demanding and certainly more valuable to humanity than a mere musician's.

He said, speaking of doctors, "We give life."

I thought that over for a moment and shot from the hip: "Yes, you do give life, but we give a reason for living."

Notes on Chapter Epigrams

Overture
Arturo Toscanini, comments made to orchestra players at La Scala and in Paris, recorded by Lily Seppilli and D. E. Ingelbrecht, published in Harvey Sach's biography *Toscanini* (Harper & Row, 1981).

Duet
David Oistrakh, an attribution by Raphael Bronstein in *The Way They Play*, Book 4 (Paganiniana).

Lessons
Robert Schumann, *House-Rules and Maxims for Young Musicians*, 1848.

Debut
Leopold Auer, *Violin Playing As I Teach It* (Stokes, 1960).

Juilliard
Maurice Ravel, *Chopin,* an essay, 1910.

Saturdays in New York
Walter Piston, *Harmony* (Norton, 1978).

Crisis
Maria Callas, on a lesson learned from conductor Tullio Serafin, in a collection of lectures, *Callas at Juilliard* (Knopf, 1987).

Naumburg
Leopold Auer, *Violin Playing As I Teach It* (Stokes, 1960).

Solo
Duke Ellington, *Music Is My Mistress* (Doubleday, 1973).

Discography of
Nadja Salerno-Sonnenberg

All recordings are on Angel Records unless otherwise noted.

Brahms
Concerto in D, Op. 77. Minnesota Orchestra, Edo de Waart. (CDC-/4DS-49429)

Sonata No. 2 in A, Op. 100. Cecile Licad, piano, (CDC-/4DS-49410)

Sonatensatz in C Minor. Cecile Licad, piano. (CDC-/4DS-49410)

Bruch
Concerto No. 1, G minor, Op. 26. Minnesota Orchestra, Edo de Waart. (CDC-/4DS-49429)

Fauré
Sonata No. 1 in A, Op. 13. Sandra Rivers, piano. Musicmasters
(MMD 60022Y)

Franck
Sonata in A. Cecile Licad, piano. (CDC-/4DS-49410)

Massenet
Méditation from *Thaïs*. New York Chamber Symphony, Gerard
Schwarz. (CDC-/DS-/4DS-49276)

Mendelssohn
Concerto in E minor, Op. 64. New York Chamber Symphony,
Gerard Schwarz. (CDC-/DS-/4DS-49276)

Prokofiev
Sonata No. 1 in F minor, Op. 80. Sandra Rivers, piano. Musicmasters (MMD 60022Y)

Saint-Saëns
Havanaise, Op. 83. New York Chamber Symphony, Gerard
Schwarz. (CDC-/DS-/4DS-49276)

Introduction and Rondo Capriccioso, Op. 28. New York Chamber Symphony, Gerard Schwarz. (CDC-/DS-/4DS-
49276)

Index